The Adventures of ERIK

by Gloria Jasperse

HOUGHTON MIFFLIN HARCOURT
School Publishers

PHOTOGRAPHY CREDITS: Cover © Didrik Johnck/CORBIS. **1** John Storey/Time Life Pictures/Getty Images. **2** courtesy of the Weihenmayer family **3** courtesy of the Weihenmayer family. **6** courtesy of the Weihenmayer family. **7** courtesy of the Weihenmayer family. **8** John Storey/Time Life Pictures/Getty Images. **9** John Storey/Time Life Pictures/Getty Images. **11** (t) courtesy of the Weihenmayer family, (b) © Didrik Johnck/Corbis. **12** (r) Todd Warshaw/Pool/Getty Images, (l) AP Photo/The White House, Paul Morse. **14** Associated Press.

Printed in China

ISBN-13: 978-0-547-01906-2
ISBN-10: 0-547-01906-8

5 6 7 8 0940 18 17 16 15 14 13 12
4500351677

Erik Weihenmayer loves a challenge. He jumps from airplanes wearing parachutes, he scuba dives in the ocean, and he climbs the tallest mountains in the world. Erik is also blind.

Erik was born with a serious illness, and there was nothing the doctors could do to stop it. The illness was making Erik go blind.

In all other ways, Erik was like any other boy. He loved the outdoors. He loved to play with his friends and family. He loved to explore, and he loved adventure.

At first, Erik could see enough to read or ride a bike if he wore very thick glasses. When he was twelve, he started to see less and less. But he refused to stop doing the things he loved. He refused to think about living in a world of darkness.

Erik in a 3-legged race

One thing Erik loved to do was ride his mountain bike. He especially liked to ride it up one ramp, fly through the air, and then land on the other ramp. But it was getting harder every day for him to do this. Erik's father watched him miss the second ramp more and more often. But instead of telling him to stop, his father painted the ramps bright orange to help Erik see them better.

Erik didn't want to stop having adventures, so he pretended he could see as well as before. But the less he could see, the harder it became to pretend.

One day, Erik went riding on his bike, but he couldn't see where he was going. Erik rode right into a tree! He knew that he couldn't pretend any longer. It was time to make a decision.

Erik decided that he could feel sorry for himself, or he could learn a new way of doing things.

A New Way of Thinking

Erik decided to learn how to do things as a blind person. His family helped. Erik's father encouraged him to think about what he could do, not what he couldn't do. And he told Erik that it was part of life to try something, fall down, and then get up and try again.

Erik learned that there were many things he could do. He could wrestle very, very well. In fact, Erik joined his high school wrestling team—and became the team captain!

Erik, age 16, with a wrestling trophy

At first it was hard for Erik to accept that he was blind. But when he had success at wrestling, he became more confident and comfortable with his blindness. He started to use a cane and learn Braille.

Erik imitated his father's way of thinking. He stopped worrying about the things he couldn't do. Instead, he began to think about the things he could do—even if they were hard. He could hike with his friends and family, and he could explore new places.

When Erik was sixteen, he discovered rock climbing. He loved the sport. He loved to think about what to do next when he climbed, and he loved the feel of the rocks and the wind.

Erik was just doing what he loved. For him, the adventures were just beginning. He was curious about the world. He wanted to explore, and he had many places he wanted to go. Later, people around the world would be amazed at his talent.

Seeking Challenges

After Erik graduated from college, he became a wrestling coach and middle school teacher. Many people were surprised that Erik could teach wrestling. They were even more surprised to learn that he had hiked in South America. They did not expect this behavior from a blind person.

In 1995, Erik climbed Denali, the highest peak in North America. Soon after that, he climbed Mount Kilimanjaro, the highest mountain in Africa. This was a very special moment for Erik. He got married on the top of that mountain! In 2001, Erik reached the summit of Mount Everest. That is the highest mountain in the world.

Still, Erik had another goal in mind. It was a goal that only 100 people had ever achieved. He would be the first blind person to do it. He wanted to climb all of the "Seven Summits"—the tallest peaks on each of the seven continents. In 2002, Erik climbed to the summit of Mount Kosciusko in Australia. He had climbed all of the Seven Summits!

Erik, his wife Ellie, and daughter Emma

Erik climbing Mount Ama Dablam

Sharing His Adventures

Erik does not live his life in silence. He has written books. He has won important awards. In 1996, Erik carried the torch at the Olympic Games. Erik has appeared in a movie and on TV. He has been on the cover of magazines. Erik is one of the greatest athletes in the world.

Erik and President Bush in 2001

But what is Erik's greatest success? Maybe it is the way he helps people who hear his story or who read it in one of his books. Erik speaks about the many things he has learned. He tells how he set himself in motion and just keeps moving forward—just as he did on his bike. He does not look back or feel bad about anything he couldn't do. Instead, he moves ahead from one adventure to the next, trying, hoping, imagining.

Erik carries Olympic Flame in 2002

Erik speaks to people all around the world. He wants them to know that they can get the knowledge they need to overcome their problems. He encourages them to follow their dreams. Erik wants them to understand that every person can do great things.

For people all around the world, Erik Weihenmayer is a hero.

Erik recites the Pledge of Allegiance at a convention in 2000.

Responding

✔ **TARGET SKILL** **Main Ideas and Details**

A main idea of this book is that Erik Weihenmayer loves adventure. Copy the chart, and add details from the story.

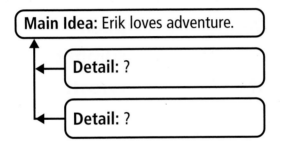

Main Idea: Erik loves adventure.

Detail: ?

Detail: ?

✎ Write About It

Text to Text Choose a person from a different book that you've read. Write a one paragraph persuasive essay to convince that person that they should or should not be adventurous. Use facts to explain your opinion.

✔ **TARGET SKILL** **Main Idea and Details** Tell important ideas and details about a topic.

✔ **TARGET STRATEGY** **Summarize** Stop to tell important ideas as you read.

GENRE A **biography** tells about events in a person's life.